Perkins County Schools
PO Box 829
Grant NE 69140-0829

At Issue

Cell Phones in Schools

Other Books in the At Issue Series:

At Issue

| Cell Phones in Schools

Roman Espejo, Book Editor

GREENHAVEN PRESS
A part of Gale, Cengage Learning

GALE
CENGAGE Learning·

Farmington Hills, Mich • San Francisco • New York • Waterville, Maine
Meriden, Conn • Mason, Ohio • Chicago

Elizabeth Des Chenes, *Director, Content Strategy*
Cynthia Sanner, *Publisher*
Douglas Dentino, *Manager, New Product*

For more information, contact:
Greenhaven Press
27500 Drake Rd.
Farmington Hills, MI 48331-3535
Or you can visit our Internet site at gale.cengage.com

For product information and technology assistance, contact us at

Gale Customer Support, 1-800-877-4253
For permission to use material from this text or product, submit all requests online at
www.cengage.com/permissions

Further permissions questions can be e-mailed to permissionrequest@cengage.com

Articles in Greenhaven Press anthologies are often edited for length to meet page requirements. In addition, original titles of these works are changed to clearly present the main thesis and to explicitly indicate the author's opinion. Every effort is made to ensure that Greenhaven Press accurately reflects the original intent of the authors. Every effort has been made to trace the owners of copyrighted material.

Cover image © Images.com/Corbis.

LIBRARY OF CONGRESS CATALOGING-IN-PUBLICATION DATA

Cell phones in schools / Roman Espejo, book editor.
     pages cm. -- (At issue)
   Includes bibliographical references and index.
   ISBN 978-0-7377-6155-9 (hardcover) -- ISBN 978-0-7377-6156-6 (pbk.)
   1. Children--Effect of technological innovations on. 2. Cell phones--Social aspects. I. Espejo, Roman, 1977- editor of compilation.
   HQ767.9.C393 2014
   302.23083--dc23
                                                                2013047113

Printed in the United States of America
1 2 3 4 5 6 7 18 17 16 15 14

Contents

Introduction

According to *Teens and Mobile Phones*, a 2010 report by the Pew Internet & American Life Project, cell phones are a "new venue for harassment and bullying" for adolescents. For instance, 26 percent of teens who have cell phones claim that someone has harassed them through their devices. Girls are more likely to be targeted at 30 percent, compared with boys at 22 percent. "This trend is more common for those teens whose parents are under 40 and low in educational attainment,"[1] the report states, which identifies prank calls, threatening or insulting calls and texts, sexual harassment, and spreading rumors as forms of bullying on cell phones.

Also in the report, teens voiced their concerns and opinions about the issue in written responses. A high school girl expressed the fear that such bullying is especially invasive, as mobile technology can be used to reach someone at any place and any time. "I think it's terrible. You can't escape the hatred. Even when you go home someone can still pick on you," she contends. Additionally, a high school boy pointed out that texting eliminates face-to-face interactions, making it easier for bullies to threaten or tease their victims. "People have bigger mouths through text," he says. Still, not all agree that bullying via cell phones is a serious problem, insisting that it is "not really a big deal."

The role of cell phones in cases of bullying and suicide has been scrutinized in recent years, paticularly following the death of Rebecca Sedwick in September 2013. Over dating a boy, the twelve-year-old middle school student from Lakeland, Florida, was taunted and intimidated by fifteen girls online and through her cell phone for more than a year. To end the

---

1. Amanda Lenhart et al., *Teens and Mobile Phones*, April 20, 2010. http://pewinternet.org /Reports/2010/Teens-and-Mobile-Phones/Chapter-5/The-cell-phone-has-become-a-new-venue-for-harassment-and-bullying-of-teens.aspx.

bullying, Sedwick's mother removed her from school, deleted her Facebook page, and took away her cell phone. Sedwick then began attending another school, showing improvement until she downloaded new mobile messaging apps. The bullying resumed. "Why are you still alive?" and "Can u die please?" are some of the messages Sedwick's bullies sent before she killed herself. "Rebecca became one of the youngest members of a growing list of children and teenagers apparently driven to suicide, at least in part, after being maligned, threatened, and taunted online, mostly through a new collection of texting and photo-sharing cell phone applications,"[2] maintains Lizette Alvarez, Miami bureau chief for *The New York Times*.

Numerous experts argue that these new mobile apps exacerbate the extent of bullying. Randy Taran, founder of youth nonprofit Project Happiness, observes that they allow bullies to remain anonymous, encouraging them to be more vicious. "In many apps and websites there is no identification or accountability for who says what. This can and does bring out the worst of human nature,"[3] she suggests. Furthermore, Taran proposes that bullies are becoming better at evading attention and punishment at school with the apps. "As teens get older, they are increasingly technologically adept and socially skillful about hiding their identity and intention," she continues. "Often these campaigns of cruelty are covert and unnoticeable by teachers, but loud and clear to both victim and their 'frenemies.'" It is also speculated that parents, including Sedwick's mother, find it nearly impossible to keep tabs on the latest apps used in bullying and monitoring their children's electronic communications. "There's a disconnect between the generations that parents are often in a constant stage of catch-

---

2. Lizette Alvarez, "Girl's Suicide Points to Rise in Apps Used by Cyberbullies," *New York Times*, September 13, 2013. http://www.nytimes.com/2013/09/14/us/suicide-of-girl-after-bullying-raises-worries-on-web-sites.html?_r=0.
3. Randy Taran, "Cyberbullying Apps—Why Are We Allowing Anonymous Cruelty?" *Huffington Post*, September 18, 2013. http://www.huffingtonpost.com/randy-taran/cyberbullying-apps_b_3941599.html.

ing up,"[4] says Kate Brodock, president of Girl Tech, an organization focusing on girls and digital media. "By the time they catch up, children are the next step ahead."

Nonetheless, other observers do not shift the blame on cell phones and apps in bullying. Ben Crompton, a British technology writer, believes that the causes are rooted in societal norms and individual behavior. "At first glance it may well appear that new technology, like smartphones and social networks, are driving this social change where bullying is rife,"[5] Crompton asserts. "However, it is far more probable that technology is shaped by social attitudes towards it, if we as a society believe it is okay for children to have smartphones they will use them as part of their normal communicative behavior." Crompton explains that a teen who is already prone to harassing his or her peers will use apps for this activity. "And if that particular child is insecure, has low self-esteem, etc., then that behavior may well result in bullying," he states. Moreover, some schools even use mobile apps to combat the problem itself. In June 2012, the Judson Independent School District in Texas released an app with a feature that allows students to report bullying and the details of the incident. The previous month, a group of students in New Haven, Connecticut, launched the Back Off Bully app, enabling users to report harassment anonymously through their smartphones, tablets, and computers. "So often, kids hide behind phones to cyberbully and do negative things,"[6] says Christine Puglisi, who led development of the Back Off Bully app. "We want them to use phones for a positive use—to start changing the world."

---

4. Quoted in NewsChannel 9, "Experts Say New Apps Increase Chances of Cyber Bullying," October 15, 2013. http://www.9wsyr.com/news/local/story/Experts-say-new-apps-increase-chances-of-cyber/h69npgUNpUGEq-oq6jFgLA.cspx.

5. Ben Crompton, "Comment: Do Mobile Phones Cause Bullying in Schools?" Pocket-lint, November 18, 2010. http://www.pocket-lint.com/news/107082-survey-mobiles-cause-bullying-schools.

6. Quoted in Melissa Bailey, "Back Off, Bully!" *New Haven Independent*, May 28, 2012. http://www.newhavenindependent.org/index.php/archives/entry/back_off_bully.

Bullying is just one of the issues raised when cell phones are welcomed on campuses. From creating a distraction in the classroom to improving academic performance to student safety, the devices and their apps polarize educators and administrators. *At Issue: Cell Phones in Schools* probes these topics and more. The divergent views presented in this anthology represent how cell phones are impacting teens as they adopt mobile technology in their daily lives.

Cell Phones Should Be Banned in Schools

Ron Kurtus

Ron Kurtus is an engineer, writer, and founder of School for Champions, an educational website.

Cell phones in and out of class are a major problem in schools and should be banned. Teachers constantly struggle with texting in class, which also distracts students from lessons. And when students receive calls in class, the ringing disrupts the entire classroom; even worse is when students answer the call, which is disrespectful to teachers and other students. Other problems include thefts of the devices and insulting texts that cause fights between students. Bans on cell phones in schools reduce both distractions and disciplinary actions, improving the environment in which teachers teach and students learn.

Many teachers have had to fight the trend of students continually sending text messages to others in and outside the classroom during class. Some students take calls on their cell phones during class or talk on their phones while walking in between classes.

Instead of requiring teachers to constantly try to maintain order, some schools have banned cell or mobile phones during school hours. The result of such a ruling has been less problems, better discipline and even a more positive school culture.

Questions you may have include:

- What are problems with cell phones in school?

- How can such problems be solved?

- What is the result of eliminating cell phones in school?

This [viewpoint] will answer those questions.

Problems with Cell Phones

In many schools—especially in more affluent areas where most students have their own cell or mobile phone—the use of the phone during class hours has become a major problem.

Texting during class. Some teachers report that they are constantly trying to stops students from sending text messages during class, especially since it is sometimes difficult to spot or detect. This is a problem among high school and college students and even among middle school students.

A student who is communicating with someone else through text messages is not paying attention and might as well not even be in the class. Although the student's grades will probably suffer and is only hurting him- or herself, the poor grades also can reflect on the instructor's ability to teach.

Another problem is some students will be sexting or sending sex text messages, which are completely inappropriate.

Getting calls in class. Teachers report that often a cell phone will ring during class, disrupting the lesson. What is worse is when the student answers the phone during class. Some will actually leave the classroom to complete their call.

Getting calls during class is not only disruptive, but it is also disrespectful to the teacher and the whole educational process.

Other cell phone problems. Other problems concerning cell phones in school concerns thefts of phones and fights as a result of insulting text messages.

Solution

Some school principals have eliminated this problem by preventing the use of cell phones—and in fact, any electronic devices such as iPods and headsets—during school. If a student's cell phone or electronics device is seen during school hours—even during lunch and break periods—it is confiscated and will only be returned when the parent comes to pick it up at the school.

The results of banning cell phones and other electronic devices in school have been dramatic in those schools which have implemented the rules.

Obviously, many students and some parents do not like such discipline, but it has been effective in schools that have implemented those rules. Going half-way often is not enough to stop the problem.

Benefits

The results of banning cell phones and other electronic devices in school have been dramatic in those schools which have implemented the rules.

Obviously, the teachers have been able to teach their classes better, without as many disruptions and the need to discipline students. Those students who got caught up in the texting fad or who would be listening to music on their iPod or similar devices not actually were learning something during class.

The removal of cell phone use during break times seemed to change the educational climate and culture of the schools. Teachers reported that students now would be seen in groups talking and some would actually be sitting and reading in common areas. This is as opposed to students communicating to others via their cell phones or text messages at that time.

Some schools reporterd a dramatic drop in behavioral referrals and the need to discipline disruptive students.

Many teachers must battle the use of texting, cell phones and electronic devices during class. Instead of requiring teachers to constantly try to maintain order, some schools have banned the use of electronic devices during school hours. The result of such a ruling has reduced problems and improved the educational culture in school.

2

Mobile Phones Poison in Schools, but Don't Blame Teachers—Blame Parents!

Frances Childs

Based in the United Kingdom, Frances Childs is a writer for the Daily Mail *and a former teacher.*

Cell phones represent much of what is wrong in schools in Great Britain. Along with gossiping, interruptions, and fighting in classrooms, teachers now face defiant students taking and receiving calls, texting, and filming one another and school staff. Furthermore, students look at pornography on cell phones, and the devices have become status symbols that cause bullying and thefts. The problem of cell phones is not with teachers—who welcome a ban on them—but with parents who want their children to be reachable at all times, or who set poor examples with inappropriate cell phone habits. Therefore, adults must discipline children and draw boundaries concerning their use of cell phones.

Holding out my hand I stare into the surly face of a large, angry teenage girl. 'Give me the phone,' I say in as calm a voice as I can muster. Truculently, 15-year-old Lisa glares at me. 'What phone?' she asks belligerently as she stuffs it back into her bag.

At this point I have a choice. I can demand that she hand the phone over; she will refuse. I can raise my voice and insist; she'll swear at me. I can give her a detention that she won't turn up to. Or I can decide not to waste any more lesson time and focus on the majority of the class who really want to learn and accept that, once again, a rude, disruptive child has scored a victory.

I make my decision. Turning my back I attempt to salvage some authority by telling Lisa not to let me see her phone again. 'What phone is that, Miss?' she sneers.

Very few teachers, especially female teachers, want to physically grapple a phone from a teenager's hand. Girls as well as boys are likely to fly off the handle and no teacher wants to provoke a violent confrontation.

And what member of staff would want to deal with the outraged parental complaint that would inevitably follow?

Forget the old-fashioned notion that a parent might actually back the teacher and berate their brazen child. As well as out-of-control pupils, the beleaguered teacher of today also has to tackle mums and dads to whom discipline is often a dirty word.

Mobile phones sum up many of the things that are wrong in schools in modern Britain. They have become, quite simply, the scourge of the classroom. That is why many teachers, like myself, will applaud yesterday's announcement by Sir Michael Wilshaw, the Chief Inspector of Schools, that pupils face a ban on mobile phones in school as part of a new Ofsted crackdown on discipline.

Schools will be penalised for failing to tackle persistent low-level disruption in lessons under a tough new inspection regime being introduced next term.

This could force heads to forbid mobile phone use by pupils—including texting, taking calls and surfing the web, often on porn sites—to avoid being marked down by inspectors.

Teachers will breathe a sigh of relief at the news, not least because mobile phones are often used to intimidate and bully both children and staff.

When I first began teaching 15 years ago, I had to cope with youngsters chatting during lessons, occasionally being rude to me and the odd fight that would flare up out of nowhere.

By the time I left the profession two years ago, things were even worse. At that point, some children were not only gossiping to each other, interrupting lessons and fighting as they always had done—they were also making and receiving calls, texting, and filming each other and members of staff.

Given that mobiles cause so much trouble, the question which needs to be asked is, why were they ever allowed in schools in the first place?

Former colleagues who are still teaching tell me that footage of them trying to keep order is played back and waved aloft in order to undermine them. I've often heard stories of mocking clips ending up on the internet for the whole world to see.

Once it became possible to surf the web on mobiles, it soon became obvious to me what many of the pupils are looking at. A friend of mine who teaches in a Manchester comprehensive told me that she has to contend with sniggering, foul comments as porn is gloated over in class with little attempt to disguise what is happening. Sometimes a phone is openly passed around. Its unpleasant and embarrassing.

'Internet porn that children view on their mobiles in school is a huge problem,' says Leonie Hodge, founder of Teen Boundaries, an anti-cyber-bullying charity that works with children in schools. 'Women on these sites are violently assaulted and raped. It's warping youngsters, especially boys, and making healthy relationships very difficult.'

Given that mobiles cause so much trouble, the question which needs to be asked is, why were they ever allowed in schools in the first place? As a teacher I never understood why they hadn't been banned. But colleagues would explain that it would take a brave teacher to run the gauntlet of angry parents who insist their children be contactable at all hours of the day and night.

If the recent experience of my friend Joanne is anything to go by, they were right. She had confiscated one girl's phone as she had been disrupting her lesson. But she hadn't even finished packing her bag at the end of the day before the girl's enraged father turned up demanding his daughter's mobile be returned.

Joanne patiently explained to him that she had decided to keep the phone until the following day as his daughter refused to turn if off in class, even accepting two calls during the lesson. 'She was chatting and laughing in my face. I simply can't have that,' Joanne told him.

Instead of apologising and assuring Joanne that he would have a word with his daughter, the father simply ratcheted up the aggression. He threatened Joanne with an official complaint and branded her a thief, before storming from the school.

Name-calling and bullying over children having the 'wrong,' phone are rife. Muggings to steal coveted models on the way to and from school are common.

As a mother myself, I understand that parents feel an extra sense of security when their children have their phones on the way to and from school. But when carried inside school, parents need to realise that phones can actually place their child in danger.

As technology has advanced, mobiles have become status symbols. Now not only do youngsters have to have the right trainers, they have to have the right phone, with all the gadgets.

Name-calling and bullying over children having the 'wrong,' phone are rife. Muggings to steal coveted models on the way to and from school are common.

And then there are the attacks on teachers themselves. One of the first attacks I witnessed in school was a fracas over a phone.

A colleague, Lydia, confiscated a phone from a teenage boy called Jason and was punched and kicked for having the temerity to do so.

This was about seven years ago, before phones had become more common in school bags than pens. Lydia was outraged when Jason got his phone out and started playing with it in the middle of a lesson.

When she demanded he hand it over, Jason grudgingly did so, but when she refused to give it back quickly enough at the end of the lesson, Jason lost his temper and lashed out.

Lydia was left terrified, seriously bruised and shocked at the level of anger directed at her. 'He just exploded,' she said.

Jason was permanently excluded—something that will have affected his whole future.

So yes, Sir Michael Wilshaw is absolutely right to target the problem of mobile phones in schools. But he is wrong to focus purely on what teachers and head teachers must do.

Parents are key to the battle. Sometimes I would call them at home and spell out just how disruptive their child's phone use was. 'Julie told me to f**ck off when I asked her to put her mobile phone away and concentrate on the lesson,' I told one mother.

'Well, the thing is, she's totally addicted to that phone,' came her mum's blithe response.

And I think the reason for attitudes like this is that the toxic influence of the mobile phone isn't confined to classrooms and teenagers. Former colleagues tell me they have noticed an increasing tendency for mums to turn up at the school gates at primary schools speaking on their phones—ignoring the little ones they haven't seen all day.

'I see them chatting away—they don't even give their five-year-olds a kiss,' one teacher in an affluent part of Sussex told me recently. 'They walk off down the street, the phone still glued to their ear.'

She has even had parents answer calls while they are speaking to her. 'Once I was talking to a mum about her son's difficulty in settling into school and she answered a phone call, leaving me standing there. I was amazed,' she recalls.

The lesson is clear. We can't just leave this problem to Sir Michael Wilshaw, heads and teachers. If we really want to stop mobile phones blighting our children's education, parents have to lead the way and reach for the 'off' button themselves.

3

Storage Services Accommodate Students Facing Cell Phone Bans

Kelly Bare

Kelly Bare is a senior editor of digital projects at the New Yorker.

Since New York City schools banned cell phones in 2005, a growing number of storage services cater to students with the devices. In more than 240 schools across the city, thousands of students risk confiscation of their cell phones by security guards because of metal detectors. Convenience stores and restaurants close by offer students "babysitting" for their devices, but storage trucks, which usually charge a dollar a day or offer weekly and monthly plans, are popping up around the city. One storage-truck service, Safe 'n' Secure Cellutions, aims to become a nonprofit to serve at-risk youth.

"*Hello Angel! Doesn't he have a great voice? I told him he's gotta start doing voice-overs. I'll be your agent, man. We can make things happen, brother.*"

"*She brings me flowers sometimes. I'm like, 'It's not gonna get you free phone storage!' It's awesome. You gotta be careful with these kids, though—make sure that you're properly handling them in a professional manner.*"

"*Where you been at, man?*"

"*I've been at home.*"

"Home is not good! You should be in school, brother!"

Jhonn de La Puente, owner of Safe 'n' Secure Cellutions, a megawatt smile, and sharp shoes, could be the most appealing man ever to spend nine hours a day, five days a week, sitting inside a vaguely ominous white cargo van.

The van—with its seven-by-fourteen-inch pass-through slot, three security cameras, and laminated Barack Obama quotes—is Puente's cell-phone-storage business. He parks it daily on Brooklyn's Washington Avenue, in between the Brooklyn Botanic Garden's new visitor center and Dr. Ronald McNair Park (named for the second African-American to travel to space, and the only one to lose his life in the Challenger explosion), earning a dollar a day from kids who attend high school across the way, on Classon Avenue.

Puente hustles. He greets each kid with a hearty "Good morning!" and demands one in return; he asks about their mood, their allergies, their truancies. He clucks if they curse in front of the window. He gets to know them one dollar at a time.

Students find many babysitters for their most precious possessions—bodegas, shoe stores, and restaurants. . . . But one-dollar-a-day device storage is a growth industry unto itself.

He once had to move the van to make way for a location shoot for "The Americans," but his gift for relationships leaves him largely undisturbed, even if he parks in front of a hydrant. Business is brisk, beginning around 7:30 A.M., with a steady stream of young faces peering through the slot until around 11 A.M. At peak times, the line stacks up six or seven students deep. He stores an average of seventy-five to a hundred devices a day.

Cell phones in schools are controversial, to the point of being a mayoral-campaign talking point. Of course, they tempt texting and exploring the delights and dangers of the Internet during class. But aren't they also vital to safety, a crucial link to family, a tool of empowerment and self-expression, a basic twenty-first-century right? The debate intensifies when you consider that the cell-phone ban, in place since 2005, is, like many things in a city with a wide gulf between rich and poor, unevenly applied. At schools with metal detectors, security guards must confiscate anything that sets them off. Elsewhere, unless you're flaunting it, your device is safe.

Students find many babysitters for their most precious possessions—bodegas, shoe stores, and restaurants, such as Sal's on Brooklyn's Franklin Avenue, where you can store free all day with the purchase of breakfast. But one-dollar-a-day device storage is a growth industry unto itself. According to a 2012 New York Civil Liberties Union survey of New York City public middle and high schools, a hundred and sixteen thousand eight hundred and seventy-four students, at two hundred and forty-two schools, go through metal detectors each day.

Pure Loyalty, in business since 2007, serves a decent chunk of them, with big blue trucks at seven schools throughout the Bronx, Manhattan, and Queens. Rates are a dollar per device per day, four dollars for the week, fifteen dollars for the month, and forty-two dollars for a three-month plan. The company refused to comment for this story, but unconfirmed reports put their revenues at around five hundred to seven hundred and fifty dollars per truck, per day, and the lines in front bear that out—as does their reported two-million-dollar insurance policy.

Safe 'n' Secure, around since 2011, is still in start-up mode.

"I thought I invented the wheel, but come to find out I didn't," says Puente. "But I can tweak it a little bit."

His tweak is a gift for customer service honed by time managing Starbucks, Fossil, and Pier 1 Imports stores, coupled with the heart of a youth outreach minister. "I want to make sure they walk out of here with a smile on their face, because a lot of these kids, you don't know what they go through at home," he says. "They're good kids, just misdirected. So you have to figure out a way to get to them."

He once put out a sign-up sheet and recruited forty kids to serve at a soup kitchen, a project he plans to repeat. He holds food drives. On "free-candy Fridays," he climbs on top of the van and tosses sweets down. He has his friend Jonathan Arnau play the guitar out front or hand out N.Y.P.D. crime-prevention pamphlets because "he's not doing anything else!" De La Puente uses the business as a platform to talk about domestic violence, catching students' interest with a poster-size picture of his sister, Xenia Puente, who died in 1997 at age sixteen.

"She was in a verbally abusive relationship that turned physical. The guy, at gunpoint, took her to the roof of a building not too far from here, actually. I don't know exactly what happened, but she ended up five stories down," he says. (The boyfriend was never charged.)

His van is paid for, as is another one, for a second location, when he can afford to staff it. Now, though, that second van holds his worldly possessions. De La Puente is, at the moment, homeless. He spends a hundred and fifty dollars a month to park the two vehicles. He showers at a Bally gym. He has a girlfriend in New Jersey, herself an entrepreneur, who does personal training via Skype. He "gets creative." "That's the sacrifice you have to make when you're an entrepreneur and you believe in something, you know?"

New customers make up a temporary four-digit PIN, which he records alongside their last name in a chart, hand-written daily in a composition book. Regulars have a customer number to go with the first letter of their last name, and the privilege of paying after school. He stores boyfriends' phones with their girlfriends', and allows them to pick up for each other.

When a manicured hand reaches through the slot and plops three devices on the narrow wooden shelf, he says, "Gimme two dollars." "I'm gonna give them a discount. I do it all the time. It keeps them coming back. They know I'm not just here to take a dollar from them."

The van is outfitted with a plywood floor, fleece blankets over the back windows, two rickety stools, a small shelf, a plastic basket overflowing with crumpled bills, and twenty-six hanging vinyl shoe-storage bags, one for each letter of the alphabet. One by one, the pockets fill up. Phones with ringing alarms prompt maddening "egg hunts."

Phones left overnight accrue a two-dollar surcharge—which he often waives. "I'm not teaching them responsibility if I don't charge them. But a lot of times I'm just a sucker." Promotional postcards stack up in your pouch if you're in arrears. At five, he makes them pay. "I don't want them to get into the habit of owing, you know?"

I'm responsible for all these phones. And the last thing I want is for someone to come to the van and I'm not there.

"Good morning, Jeanette! Ask me the question you ask me everyday."

"I ask him if his bladder is O.K."

"She cracks me up with that every single time."

"I never lock up and leave, no way. I'm petrified. I'm responsible for all these phones. And the last thing I want is for someone to come to the van and I'm not there. Word gets around really quick."

In the winter, Puente runs the van all day, to keep the heat on and his laptop charged. He passes the time studying business administration online, or reading. A dog-eared copy of Junot Díaz's "Drown" lies on the console between the two front seats.

Or he'll do other business: editing photos, or video, like "Mothers of No Tomorrow," a 2013 documentary about black-on-black violence that he made with his friend Nicholas "Sixx" King, with whom he used to crash award shows.

Puente initially thought he might get the schools to pay for his services. "I wrote up a proposal and everything, but it was a conflict of interest with the D.O.E., because by law these kids are not allowed to bring these devices into school, so they can't cut a check to me."

Now, his "four-year plan" involves going nonprofit. "You don't get elevated in this life by just looking out for yourself." Just this week, he started a Kickstarter campaign.

After the pickup rush, at 4 P.M., plus "a five-minute grace period," he closes up shop and goes to get his own kids, Jah'Shua, age eleven, and Jah'Naya, seven, who spend a couple hours doing homework and hanging out before he drops them off at their mom's house.

That business hours match his kids' schedules is a plus. Soon enough, they'll be teen-agers clamoring for smartphones of their own. And, like most of de la Puente's clients—and people of all ages, everywhere—loathe to part with them for even an instant. Or maybe they'll be in the philosophical minority, like Sheba Baptiste, age fifteen, who says she doesn't really miss her phone during the day. "It's kind of a good thing for me, to have a break."

4

Campus Safety Must Be Considered if Cell Phones Are Allowed in Schools

National School Safety and Security Services

Based in Cleveland, Ohio, National School Safety and Security Services is a firm that provides assessments and training in school security, emergency planning, and crisis response.

In light of school shootings and the 2001 terrorist attacks, allowing students to carry cell phones in schools for their safety has become a matter of debate among school administrators, parents, and students. If the devices are permitted, schools must realistically adapt to the implications for the campus environment, safety, and security. Overall, cell phones are disruptive in the classroom. Moreover, students' phone use during an emergency can actually undermine safety; calls to parents can overload phone systems, parents flocking to schools can hinder emergency response and place themselves in danger, and texting can spread rumors about the situation. Whatever their policies on cell phones, schools must clearly and consistently enforce them and set strong emergency guidelines and crisis communications planning into place.

National School Safety and Security Services has received a number of inquiries after school shootings over the years asking if schools should allow and/or encourage students to carry cell phones in school as a tool for their safety during a school shooting or other crisis. Similar inquiries were received after the Columbine High School attack in 1999 and the September 2001 terrorist attacks on America. We set forth [in this viewpoint] a look at the historical perspective of cell phones in schools, a detailed explanation of how they can detract from safety in a crisis, and recommendations for addressing the current day reality of cell phones and other technology being a part of today's students' lives and how schools must adapt realistically.

Historical Perspectives

For more than a decade we opposed policies allowing or encouraging students to have cell phones in school. On a day-to-day basis, they are disruptive to the educational environment. This also has been the general position of many school districts over the years. Changing policies under the guise of cell phones being a crisis tool for student safety for a very long time was, in our opinion, driven more by parental and student convenience issues than safety.

Some schools banned pagers and cell phones starting a decade ago because of their connection to drug and gang activity, as well as due to the disruption to classes. The focus on their disruption of the educational process has come into conflict, though, with the reality of cell phones becoming a common convenience item and part of everyone's daily life. However, parents have increasingly lobbied boards to change policies primarily based on the argument that phones will make students and schools safer in light of national tragedies, and we believe there needs to be a clear understanding of how cell phone use during a tragedy can detract from school safety and create a less safe environment.

Times evolve, however, and technology certainly evolves. Cell phones, I-pads, digital gaming, and other technology is being integrated into the day-to-day learning experience of many students in schools across the nation. The methods in which they communicate (email, texting, instant messaging, etc.) and the tools to do so are readily available in so many forms. Having technology in schools as instructional tools, and believing one can simultaneously eliminate the ability of students to communicate electronically with each other and the outside community, appears to be increasingly unrealistic thinking. So our thoughts on cell phones in schools must adapt to the times.

The use of cell phones by students during a bomb threat, and specifically in the presence of an actual explosive device, also may present some risk for potentially detonating the device.

But first let's look at the climate, safety, and crisis angles....

Cell Phones Disruptive of School Environment

From an educational perspective, cell phone use during classes and in other areas of the school can easily present a disruption to the educational environment on a day-to-day basis.

School disruptions can come in a number of forms. Ringing cell phones can disrupt classes and distract students who should be paying attention to their lessons at hand. Text message has been used for cheating. And new cell phones with cameras could be used to take photos of exams, take pictures of students changing clothes in gym locker areas, and so on.

Cell Phone Use During a Crisis Can Disrupt School Emergency Response

In terms of school safety, cell phones have been used by students in a number of cases nationwide for calling in bomb threats to schools. In far too many cases, these threats have been difficult or impossible to trace since they have been made by cell phones. The use of cell phones by students during a bomb threat, and specifically in the presence of an actual explosive device, also may present some risk for potentially detonating the device as public safety officials typically advise school officials not to use cell phones, two-way radios, or similar communications devices during such threats.

Additionally, experience in crisis management has shown us that regular school telephone systems become overloaded with calls in times of a crisis. While we do recommend cell phones for school administrators and crisis team members as a crisis management resource tool, it is highly probable that hundreds (if not thousands) of students rushing to use their cell phones in a crisis would also overload the cell phone system and render it useless. Therefore the use of cell phones by students could conceivably decrease, not increase, school safety during a crisis.

Cell phone use, texting, and other outside communications by students during a crisis also expedites parental flocking to the school at a time when school and public safety officials may need parents to be away from the school site due to evacuations, emergency response, and/or other tactical or safety reasons. This could also actually delay or otherwise hinder timely and efficient parent-student reunification. In extreme situations, it could thrust parents into a zone of potential harm.

Cell phone use also accelerates the unintentional (and potentially intentional) spread of misinformation, rumors, and fear.

Cell Phones and Text Messaging in Schools Contribute to Rumors and Fear

We also track more and more school incidents across the nation where rumors have disrupted schools and have even resulted in decreased attendance due to fears of rumored violence. The issues of text messaging in particular, and cell phones in general, were credited with sometimes creating more anxiety and panic than any actual threats or incidents that may have triggered the rumors.

"We are now dealing with 'Generation Text' instead of 'Generation X'," said Ken Trump, President of National School Safety and Security Services. "The rumors typically become greater than the issue, problem, or incident itself. Attendance can go down overnight and rumors can fly in minutes," he noted.

Ken's advice to school and safety officials includes:

1. Anticipate you will have an issue that catches fire like this at some time. Identify ahead of time what mechanisms you will use to counter it.

2. Have redundancy in communications: Web site, direct communications to students and staff, mass parent notifications, letters to go home, etc.

3. Discuss some potential scenarios with your district and building administrators and crisis teams to evaluate what the threshold will be for going full speed on your response communications. If you go full speed on every single rumor, you might need two full-time employees just to counter rumors in one average secondary school. Try to get a feel for at what point a situation might rise to the level of being so disruptive or distractive that it warrants a full-fledged communications counter assault by school and police officials.

4. School and police officials should have unified communications so as to send consistent messages. We train in our emergency preparedness programs for the use of joint information centers (JICs) in a major critical incident response. But even on lower scale incidents, it is

important for school leaders to be sending a message consistent with that of public safety officials to their school-communities.

5. Have a formal crisis communications plan and professionally train your administrators and crisis team members on communicating effectively with media and parents. Professional outside communications consultants, district communications staff (for those with such in-house resources), and related specialists can help develop and audit communications plans, and train staff.

Having technology in schools as instructional tools, and believing one can simultaneously eliminate the ability of students to communicate electronically with each other and the outside community, appears to be increasingly unrealistic thinking.

"The key is to be prepared to fight fire with fire. Today's high-tech world and rapid communications must be countered by school officials who have a solid communications plan for managing rapidly escalating rumors around school safety issues," Trump said. . . .

Cell Phones and Other Technology as Instructional Tools

As noted earlier above, times evolve and technology use certainly evolves with them. Cell phones, I-pads, digital gaming, and other technology is being integrated into the day-to-day learning experience of many students in schools across the nation. We have seen exceptionally impressive engaged learning in schools with one-to-one technology where kids from kindergarten grade on up have I-pads or laptop computers. One superintendent commented that in his more than 40 years in education, he has never seen kids so engaged in learning.

The methods in which they communicate (email, texting, instant messaging, etc.) and the tools to do so are readily available in so many forms. Having technology in schools as instructional tools, and believing one can simultaneously eliminate the ability of students to communicate electronically with each other and the outside community, appears to be increasingly unrealistic thinking. We must therefore provide more time-relevant recommendations than in the past where simply recommending a ban on devices was realistic and practical.

Cell Phone Policies and Practices in Schools Must Be Consistent

School boards and administrators have the final say in whether cell phones are or are not banned in their schools. We respect local control and their right to make these decisions. If a school district chooses to ban cell phones, we support that as we support those districts choosing to allow students to have cell phones in schools.

We now strongly encourage school districts to have crisis communications plans to manage and respond in a timely manner to rumors and to communicate on security incidents and in crises.

We do believe, however, that school leaders must make a firm decision, set it in written policy, implement it consistently, and communicate expectations to students, parents, and school employees. Equally important is that they enforce their policies in a firm, fair, and consistent manner for the long haul. Saying in writing that the district bans cell phones but in practice allowing them or having a "don't ask, don't tell" practice day-to-day is unacceptable.

School administrators allowing students to possess and/or in some fashion use cell phones in schools and/or on school property must provide clear guidelines and expectations to students and parents. They must [enforce] them consistently.

Crisis Communication Plans Must Address Cell Phone Usage

From a safety, security, and emergency/crisis preparedness perspective, school boards, administrators, crisis teams, and public safety officials must have a detailed conversation on the impact of cell phones on day-to-day school climate, their potential adverse impact on security, and their high-risk for detracting from efficient school emergency response and management in a critical incident. We now strongly encourage school districts to have crisis communications plans to manage and respond in a timely manner to rumors and to communicate on security incidents and in crises. We also advise school and safety officials to develop their emergency plans with the expectation that cell phone use in a criticial incident will accelerate rumors, expedite parental and other flocking to the school, create traffic and human movement management problems, potentially hinder efficient parent-student reunification processes, etc. In short, school and safety officials must "double-down" on their planning and preparedness for issues likely to be created by cell phone use during a crisis.

School leaders should talk with students, parents, and staff about their expectations regarding cell phone use during a crisis. There should be candid discussions of how cell phone use can hurt school and first responder efforts to keep students and staff safe during an emergency. And students, parents, and staff should be told how responsible use and non-use during a crisis can help make the situation more safe and less risky than irresponsible use and use at critical times when attention should be given fully to receiving directions from those responsible for keeping everyone safe.

School leaders should maintain an adequate number of cell phones on campus for administrators, crisis team members, and other appropriate adults. School and safety officials should seek to provide such equipment as a part of their crisis planning. Additionally, while not necessarily advocating that schools provide cell phones to teachers, we do believe that school policies should allow teachers and support staff to carry their cell phones if they choose to do so.

Concluding Thoughts

Technology evolves. Society evolves. And so must our thinking on the role of technology, cell phones and other technology in schools. Regardless of whether or not school leaders formally allow or prohibit student cell phones on campus, they must have preparedness plans designed upon the assumption that at least some students will have and use cell phones during a crisis situation. Emergency preparedness guidelines and crisis communications plans must be in place to respond to and manage such conditions.

5

Students Have a Right to Privacy if Their Cell Phones Are Confiscated

Student Press Law Center

Founded in 1974, Student Press Law Center (SPLC) advocates the constitutional rights of high school and college journalists and open government on campuses.

Many schools restrict students' use of cell phones, with some banning possession of the devices. However, the Fourth Amendment restricts the search and seizure of students' property unless there is "reasonable suspicion" that evidence of a legal or school violation will be found. Students should understand their schools' search and seizure policies and demand changes if they are unconstitutional. In addition, student journalists should be aware of how their confidential materials and news sources are protected. If their cell phones are searched, students cannot obstruct the search, but can refuse consent and question the reasons for it as well as request a consultation with parents or an attorney.

Schools throughout the country have adopted policies restricting the use of cell phones during the school day, including some that ban possession of the phones entirely. While a school has leeway to decide how and when phones may be used, the Fourth Amendment to the Constitution restricts the ability of any government agency—including a public school—to seize a person's property or search the contents of that property, including a phone. Journalists who use their phones for recording news may have some additional protection under federal law as well.

Protecting your legal rights starts with understanding what the law does and does not protect, and learning how to intelligently assert your rights without crossing the line into defiance or disruption.

Dos and Don'ts

Before a Search —Do make sure you understand your school's policy regarding searches. Taking the time to read and think over your school's policy ahead of time allows you to think about whether the policy is consistent with your constitutional rights.

—Do advocate for a policy change if you believe your school's policy infringes on your rights. The Fourth Amendment provides that, while at a public school (which includes charter schools), students must be free from searches and seizures unless school administrators can show that they had a "reasonable suspicion" that the search would turn up evidence of a violation of a specific state law, or of a school rule or policy. In other words, a school cannot simply "go fishing" into people's phone messages in hopes that a rule violation might turn up.

—Do work with the news media—both on-campus and in the community—to publicize parts of the policy that you feel violate your rights. Research and write about how these policies affect you and your fellow students.

If you are searched —Do understand that you may refuse to consent to a search of yourself and/or your possessions at any time. Consider asking for an opportunity to consult a parent or an attorney, or to have a parent present. Understand, however, that even if you withhold consent, school officials may still conduct a search if they are aware of facts that would provide reasonable grounds to do so. Importantly, your refusal cannot be used as evidence that you have something to hide or as evidence that there are reasonable grounds to search you.

—Don't attempt to interfere with the search while it is being conducted. Even if you have refused consent, you may not interfere with an ongoing search.

—Do maintain a calm and polite tone at all times.

—Don't lie. Furnishing false information will only hurt your ability to defend yourself. Even if you have broken the law or school rules, evidence from the search probably cannot be used against you if the search is found to be illegal.

Consult with an attorney if you believe that your rights were violated and the school is unresponsive to your complaints.

After the search —Do write down the details of the search as soon as you can, including everything that was said and who was present or who witnessed it. If other people have been searched, have them document everything they can remember as well.

—Do ensure that school authorities complied with any written policies your school has, and do make note of instances where the search or seizure strayed from the school's written policy.

—Do complain to higher authorities within the school if you feel that you were searched in violation of your constitutional rights. Write to your school board or contact your superintendent to complain.

—Do consult with an attorney if you believe that your rights were violated and the school is unresponsive to your complaints.

For Student Journalists

—A federal law, the Privacy Protection Act [PPA], forbids the police from searching for a journalist's confidential materials without a court order. If you are a student journalist whose cell phone contains recordings of interviews, or text messages between you and a confidential news source, then you probably are covered by the PPA if the police demand your phone (though it's unclear whether the law will help if the demand comes from a teacher or principal). If your phone is taken away, mention the Privacy Protection Act and your rights as a journalist to put the police on notice.

—If your school has a strict cell phone policy, be mindful that being a journalist gives you no special rights to break rules. If you are keeping confidential newsgathering material on a phone that you know is "contraband" on campus, you are living dangerously. Consider using something safer. . . .

The authority to take away a phone is not the same as the authority to search what is recorded on it.

Students Must Remember Rules

—Many students are understandably upset when schools search their possessions. They feel that their privacy has been invaded, and they want to protest. Nevertheless, it is critical to remain calm at all times during a search, no matter how much you believe the school is breaking the law. At no point during the search should you resist or try to interfere with or obstruct the search.

—Although you may not obstruct the search, you may refuse to consent to it, and you may also question the reasons for the search. Keep in mind that if you are searched outside of school by law enforcement, the police must show "probable cause" before you or your possessions may be searched. If you are in school, however, a lower standard applies: school officials need only "reasonable suspicion" that a search of your belongings will lead them to evidence that you have violated a relevant law or school rule.

—The authority to take away a phone is not the same as the authority to search what is recorded on it. Even if the school is within its legal authority to confiscate a phone, searching the contents of the phone is not allowed unless there is reason to believe the phone contains evidence of illegal or prohibited behavior.

—School rules and policies do not trump the Constitution. If the school insists that it need not follow the Constitution because it is bound by school policy, then the school is wrong. A policy that is inconsistent with the Constitution is legally void.

—The Constitution does not give you any special rights to insist on having or using a cell phone on campus. It protects you only against unreasonable seizures and searches.

6

A Is for App: Smartphones, Handheld Computers Sparked Revolution

Anya Kamenetz

Anya Kamenetz is a contributing writer for Fast Company *and was nominated for the Pulitzer Prize in Feature Writing in 2005. She is also the author of* DIY U: Edupunks, Edupreneurs, and the Coming Transformation of Higher Education.

The current generation of children will not know of a world without mobile technology, and much of the time they spend consuming and creating media will be on smartphones. As tools of interaction and expression, handhelds are helping kids learn, as seen in the latest studies and pilot projects spreading across the country. One device in particular, TeacherMate, is not only improving math and reading skills of elementary school students with innovative games but also offers cutting-edge educational programs to children in poor, isolated regions worldwide. Some critics raise concerns about the "iTeach" future—such as the continued reliance on simpler, cheaper technologies and commercialization of mobile learning—but smartphones and handhelds have the potential to revolutionize education.

Gemma and Eliana Singer are big iPhone fans. They love to explore the latest games, flip through photos, and watch YouTube videos while waiting at a restaurant, having their hair done, or between ballet and French lessons. But the Manhattan twins don't yet have their own phones, which is good, since they probably wouldn't be able to manage the monthly data plan: In November, they turned 3.

When the Singer sisters were just 6 months old, they already preferred cell phones to almost any other toy, recalls their mom, Fiona Aboud Singer: "They loved to push the buttons and see it light up." The girls knew most of the alphabet by 18 months and are now starting to read, partly thanks to an iPhone app called First Words, which lets them move tiles along the screen to spell *c-o-w* and *d-o-g*. They sing along with the Old MacDonald app too, where they can move a bug-eyed cartoon sheep or rooster inside a corral, and they borrow Mom's tablet computer and photo-editing software for a 21st-century version of finger painting. "They just don't have that barrier that technology is hard or that they can't figure it out," Singer says.

A Generation Adept at Handheld and Networked Technology

Gemma and Eliana belong to a generation that has never known a world without ubiquitous handheld and networked technology. American children now spend 7.5 hours a day absorbing and creating media—as much time as they spend in school. Even more remarkably, they multitask across screens to cram 11 hours of content into those 7.5 hours. More and more of these activities are happening on smartphones equipped with audio, video, SMS [short message service], and hundreds of thousands of apps.

The new connectedness isn't just for the rich. Mobile adoption is happening faster worldwide than that of color TV a half-century ago. Mobile-phone subscribers are expected to hit

5 billion during 2010; more than 2 billion of those live in developing countries, with the fastest growth in Africa. Mobile broadband is forecast to top access from desktop computers within five years.

New studies and pilot projects show smartphones can actually make kids smarter.

As with television, many people are wondering about the new technology's effect on children. "The TV set was pretty much a damned medium back in the '60s," says Gary Knell, CEO [chief executive officer] of Sesame Workshop. But where others railed against the "vast wasteland," *Sesame Street* founders Joan Ganz Cooney and Lloyd Morrisett saw a new kind of teacher. "They said, Why don't we use it to teach kids letters and numbers and get them ready for school?" *Sesame Street*, from its 1969 debut, changed the prevailing mind-set about a new technology's potential. With its diverse cast and stoop-side urban setting, the show was aimed especially at giving poor kids a head start on education.

Today, handheld and networked devices are at the same turning point, with an important difference: They are tools for expression and connection, not just passive absorption. "You put a kid in front of a TV, they veg out," says Andrew Shalit, creator of the First Words app and father of a toddler son. "With an iPhone app, the opposite is true. They're figuring out puzzles, moving things around using fine motor skills. What we try to do with the game is create a very simple universe with simple rules that kids can explore."

For children born in the past decade, the transformative potential of these new universes is just beginning to be felt. New studies and pilot projects show smartphones can actually make kids smarter. And as the search intensifies for technological solutions to the nation's and the world's education woes—"Breakthrough Learning in a Digital Age," as the title of a summit at Google HQ [headquarters] last fall [2009] had it—growing sums of money are flowing into the sector. The U.S. Department of Education has earmarked $5 billion in competitive school-reform grants to scale up pilot programs and evaluate best practices of all kinds. Major foundations are specifically zeroing in on handhelds for preschool and the primary grades. "Young kids and multisensor-touch computing are a huge area of innovation," says Phoenix Wang, the head of a startup philanthropic venture fund called Startl—funded by the Gates, MacArthur, and Hewlett foundations—that's entirely focused on educational investing. Google, Nokia, Palm, and Sony have all supplied handheld devices for teaching. Thousands of new mobiles—not just smartphones but also ever-shrinking computers—have come into use at schools in the United States and around the world just in the past year.

To understand the transformative potential—and possible pitfalls—of this device-driven instructional reboot, you can look at the impact of one machine, the TeacherMate, that is getting educational futurists excited. It has the total package of appropriate design, quality software, and an ability to connect kids with teachers and technologists. And while it will have to leap huge hurdles—systemic, bureaucratic, cultural—to be widely adopted, it does present the tantalizing prospect of revolutionizing how children are educated by drawing on their innate hunger to seize learning with both hands and push all the right buttons.

"It Doesn't Feel Like Homework"

When I walk into the first-grade classroom at Henry Clay Elementary School on Chicago's South Side, the lights are off and the room is silent. Three-quarters of the 20 children are plugged into headphones, staring into little blue machines. The TeacherMate, as it is called, is a handheld computer with a four-hour battery life. It runs full-color Flash games on a platform partly open to volunteer developers worldwide, and it can record and play back audio. Julissa Muñoz shyly tells me that she likes this device better than her PlayStation 2 at home. "They have lots of games," she says. "I like the fireman game," where exciting music plays as you choose the right length ladder, which sneakily teaches simple addition and subtraction.

The kids like the TeacherMate because it gives them a feeling of freedom.

Julissa's teacher, the delightfully named Kelly Flowers, explains that the software on her laptop lets her track each student's performance. Once a week, when she plugs each student's TeacherMate into her docking station, she downloads a record of their game play and generates reports for herself as well as for parents. Then she sets the precise skills, levels, and allotted time for the upcoming week. The programs are synced with the reading and math curricula used in the school—right down to the same spelling words each week.

Most important, says Flowers, the TeacherMate works. She privately sorts her kids into three groups based on their reading skills—green (scoring at or above grade level), yellow (borderline), and red (underperformers). "This year, with TeacherMate, I started with 11 greens, 2 yellows, and 7 reds. By the middle of the year, I had just 2 reds. I can move a red to a yellow on my own, but this is my first year moving a red directly to a green. I've never seen that much growth in that short a time." Flowers's observations are backed up by preliminary University of Illinois research that suggests that reading and math scores in classrooms with TeacherMates are significantly higher than in those without.

Flowers says the kids like the TeacherMate because it gives them a feeling of freedom. "It doesn't feel like homework," she says. "They can choose from a whole list of games. They don't know that I decided what [skills] they'd be working on." And during the time her class spends with TeacherMates each day, Flowers can devote more focused time and attention to small groups of students.

Transforming Schooling in America with Technology

TeacherMate is the brainchild of a bearded technology lawyer turned social entrepreneur from Evanston, Illinois, named Seth Weinberger, who punctuates his verbal volleys with waving hands and liberal profanity. He says he's on year 15 of a 30-year personal life plan to transform schooling in America using technology.

Innovations for Learning worked with a Chinese company to cheaply design and develop the TeacherMate, which debuted in 2008.

When Weinberger's daughter and son, now college-age, were toddlers, he and his wife helped start a preschool. "I donated some computers and was going to donate some reading software," he says. "I went to Best Buy in 1993 and I couldn't see how any of the stuff they had could teach a kid anything." At his law firm, Weinberger happened to have some video-game designers as clients; he asked them to create a game-based reading program. It was a hit. "The school loves it, I love it. To me, this is the future of education. I go back to the clients and say, 'This is a great beginning!' They say, 'No, this is the great ending. There's no market for educational software.'"

Weinberger disagreed, and decided to teach himself how to program. He would work from 8 a.m. to 8 p.m. at the law firm, go home, and work from 9 p.m. to 2 a.m. at his computer—his obsession with education making him a near-absentee dad to his own kids. Eventually, he licensed the software, which allowed him to "hire real developers who rewrote everything, laughing hysterically," he says.

For the next 12 years, Weinberger continued to develop K-2 level reading and math software through his not-for-profit, Innovations for Learning, coordinating the work of programmers in India and Argentina with teachers at a dozen schools in Chicago. Three years ago, Weinberger and his team realized handheld mobile devices had gotten sophisticated enough to be ideal for classroom use. They were cheaper and more durable than laptops, and teachers found their smaller size proved less distracting in class. Moreover, he says, kids seemed to intuitively understand how to use the simpler machines. "We encourage teachers not to do any pretraining," he says. "Pass them out, turn them on, and have the kid start."

Existing PDAs [personal digital assistants] such as the PalmPilot and Dell Axim, on initial testing, proved a little too delicate and expensive for classroom use. So Innovations for Learning worked with a Chinese company to cheaply design and develop the TeacherMate, which debuted in 2008. Currently, it sells for $100, bundled with games customized to match each of the major K-2 reading and math curricula. . . .

Pocket School

Late on Thanksgiving night, I'm in a van bumping over gravel roads in Baja California, Mexico, with Paul Kim, the chief technology officer of Stanford University's School of Education; a field team of four students; and two boxes of Teacher-Mates. Stray dogs prowl in front of roadside taquerias, their eyes glowing red in our passing headlights. Noah Freedman, a 19-year-old Princeton sophomore, is on his laptop in the front seat doing some last-minute debugging of an interactive storytelling program, while Ricardo Flores, a Stanford master's student, translates the software's directions into Spanish— giving a new meaning, Freedman jokes, to "mobile development."

We spend the next two days meeting with Mixtec and Zapotec children at *campos*, farm workers' camps with rows of corrugated-steel-roofed barracks set on packed mud. We roll into the compounds in the back of a truck driven by a local missionary and hand out bags of rice and beans to the mothers, who tell me that the youth here—clad in the international uniform of hoodies, jeans, and sneakers—are struggling with borderlands issues of drugs and violence on top of rural poverty and isolation. And though schools here are supposed to run in half-day sessions, we find schoolhouses empty and locked both morning and afternoon.

Kim is devoted to using cell phones to provide poor children with the basics of education and with access to all of the world's information. "Kids love stories," he says. "In places with no TV, no Internet, no books, when they are given these devices, these are like gifts from heaven." He has long dreamed of a machine that is cheap, powered with a solar or bicycle charger, and equipped with game-based learning content—a complete "Pocket School." For the past four years, he has been testing phones from a dozen different manufacturers, but the TeacherMate, which he discovered in March 2008, comes closer than anything to the Pocket School ideal.

The more you expect from a kid, the smarter they're going to get.

The Mexico trip is one of a whirlwind of small user-testing and demonstration projects that Kim has undertaken in the past 12 months. He has personally brought TeacherMates to Rwanda, Uganda, Kenya, India, South Korea, Costa Rica, the Philippines, Palestine, and several sites in Mexico, in most cases working with local not-for-profits, trying them out for a few hours and on a few dozen children at a time. He brings along programmers, like Freedman, so they can get feedback and tweak the software accordingly. In South Korea, Mexico, and the Philippines, schools and community centers continue to use the devices and collect data.

Letting Kids Figure It Out by Themselves

Kim's TeacherMate strategy, like Weinberger's, is to let the kids figure it out by themselves. In Baja, I watch children aged 6 to 12 pick the machine up and within a few minutes, with no direct instructions, they're working in groups of three, helping one another figure out the menus in English by trial and error, playing the same math games as the students in Chicago, and reading along with stories in Spanish. The children agree that the TeacherMates are *bonitas*—"cute." An 11-year-old named Silvia asks me hopefully, "*Son regalos?*" ("Are these gifts?") I have to say that they are only for borrowing. The missionary, Pablo Ohm, will keep the TeacherMates at the community center he runs in the town of Camalu, but access won't be regular.

One of Kim's inspirations was [African American scientist] George Washington Carver, who brought a "movable school"—a horse-drawn wagon full of agricultural exhibits—to poor black communities in rural Alabama in the 1920s. Kim is targeting especially the kids whose circumstances make it impossible to attend school regularly: refugees, migrants, the homeless. "Unesco reports that there are 150 million street children and another 250 million who will never see a book," he says. "Donating books is great, but think about it. When you mail a book from here to Rwanda, the shipping will cost you way more than the cost of the book, and maybe nobody there can read the book."

Whereas Weinberger wants to improve teaching practices at existing schools, Kim focuses overwhelmingly on empowering kids to teach themselves. He sees technology as a liberating force, helping kids in rich and poor countries alike bypass schools, with all their waste, bureaucracy, and failures, entirely. "Why does education need to be so structured? What are we so afraid of?" he asks. "The more you expect from a kid, the smarter they're going to get." . . .

The iTeach Future

Mobile phones have transformed communications, especially in the developing world, more swiftly than anyone could have imagined. The prospect of doing the same for education—putting best-of-breed learning software in kids' hands anytime, anywhere—is tantalizing. Yet not everyone is so excited about what might be called the iTeach future.

The same possibilities that make these technologies so exciting . . . make them threatening to the educational status quo.

While a $100 curriculum-in-a-box may seem like a good value even by developing-country standards, wide distribution would still be costly. Many experts maintain that educational interventions in the poorest countries should stick to even cheaper technologies that have already proven their value, like chalkboards and paper. "Before one can make use of a computer, reading and writing are fundamentals," says Erin Ganju, CEO of the social enterprise Room to Read, which has built and stocked 9,000 developing-world libraries over the past decade with plain old paper books. "For as little as $5 a year per child, we can create a well-stocked library with a trained librarian."

And then there is the anticommercialization camp. Skeptics are wary about the motives of cell-phone makers and telecom-service providers, which would reap a windfall should governments embrace mobile learning—Unesco has estimated educational spending worldwide at $2.5 trillion annually. And as with the boob tube before it, there's worry that wide adoption of mobile technologies for learning will give marketers direct access to a very impressionable demographic. "Cell phones are increasingly a way for advertisers to target children," says Josh Golin of the Campaign for a Commercial-Free Childhood. "We've seen branded Burger King games downloaded to cell phones and text-message advertising sent to kids."

But the biggest challenge to Pocket School–style learning may not be the business model. The same possibilities that make these technologies so exciting—the sight of Gemma, Eliana, Julissa, and Silvia pushing the buttons, controlling their own learning and their own destiny—make them threatening to the educational status quo. A system built around tools that allow children to explore and figure things out for themselves would be radical for most developing-world schools, which emphasize learning by rote. In the United States, which is currently so in love with state curriculum benchmarks and standardized tests, it could be just as hard a sell.

What's at issue is a deep cultural shift, a fundamental rethinking not only of how education is delivered but also of what "education" means. The very word comes from the Latin *duco*, meaning "to lead or command"—putting the learner in the passive position. Rabi Kamacharya is an MIT [Massachusetts Institute of Technology] engineering grad who returned to his native Kathmandu from Silicon Valley to found a software company and started OLE Nepal, the network's most established branch, in 2007. Kamacharya talks about technology putting "children in the driver's seat"—to overcome the limited skills of teachers: "Even in urban areas, teachers who teach English, for example, do not know English very well. Children are at the mercy of the teachers, who may not be motivated or have sufficient materials to work with. We want to enable them to go forward with self-learning and assessment."

This idea, common among these tech-driven educational entrepreneurs, imagines a new role for teachers. "The main transformational change that needs to happen is for the teacher to transform from the purveyor of information to the coach," says Weinberger of Innovations for Learning. . . .

The challenge of putting such ideas into practice—and getting the kids into the educational driver's seat—is so daunting it's almost laughable. Still, when you've seen a tiny child eagerly embracing a device that lets her write, draw, figure out math, and eventually find an answer to any question she might ask, it's hard not to feel the excitement of the moment, or its revolutionary potential. We're talking about leapfrogging over massive infrastructure limitations to unleash what Kim calls "the only real renewable resource"—the inventive spark of 1 billion children. "They're creative, these children," he says, "no matter where they are."

7

Smartphones Do Not Benefit Classroom Learning

Maclean's

Maclean's *is a Canadian weekly news magazine.*

Smartphones offer several advantages in an educational setting, such as the electronic delivery of textbooks and other learning materials to students and linking classmates together with communication technology. Nonetheless, with the temptations to text, surf the Internet, and log onto social networks, mobile devices are also "tools of mass distraction" in the classroom. While smartphones can lower educational costs and enhance student satisfaction, they are not shown to improve academic performance; thus it is too soon to advocate their use in educational settings. Ultimately, technology cannot replace the vital skills of teachers to challenge the minds and capture the attention of distracted students.

The role of technology in the classroom has no doubt been a contentious issue since the first Roman student brought an abacus to his grammaticus. Using the most up-to-date equipment in school has always seemed to be a necessity. And yet the process of learning hasn't really changed that much since ancient times: teachers still need to teach and students still need to pay attention.

Last week [September 2010] Ontario Premier Dalton McGuinty sparked a national debate on the role of technology in Canadian classrooms. Asked about a proposal to relax a ban on cellphones in the classrooms of Toronto-area high schools, the premier seemed rather agreeable to the idea. "Telephones, BlackBerries and the like are conduits for information and one of the things we want our students to be is well informed," he said. "It's something we should be looking at in our schools."

McGuinty has a point. It seems inevitable that some sort of hand-held wireless device will eventually become part of education systems across the country. The cost and complication of traditional textbooks makes electronic delivery of course material straight into the hands of students a rather attractive proposition. For this reason alone, electronic tablets or smartphones such as the BlackBerry likely have a place in the classroom of the future. The prospect of linking students together via communication technology also holds great educational promise.

Tools of Mass Distraction

At the same time, we can't ignore the enormous and obvious downsides of such technological intrusions. Cellphones may be conduits for information, but they're also tools of mass distraction. Texting, tweeting, surfing and updating your online profile have nothing to do with learning and no place in the classroom. Yet it's even become commonplace for parents to text their children during school hours. What are they thinking?

Any effort to make cellphones part of the official school day must solve the problem of their non-educational use, either by setting strict rules of acceptable conduct or blocking access when it's not appropriate. And we should recognize that there's a big difference between integrating wireless devices into the curriculum and simply inviting students to bring whatever diverting gadgets they might possess to class. The fact not every student owns a smartphone must also be addressed. Regardless of what the future holds, it's far too soon to be advocating widespread use of cellphones in the classroom.

Oversold by Advocates

It's also the case that the value of technology to learning is frequently oversold by eager advocates. A long series of educational revolutions via technology has been promised throughout the years: from television to video to desktop computers to laptops to SMART Boards to cellphones. Despite claims that these innovations will change the educational experience for the better, there's no evidence technology actually leads to higher marks for students.

The smartest phones may be the ones we keep outside the classroom.

The ubiquitous presence of wireless laptops on university campuses in many ways anticipates the presence of cellphones in public schools. A study from 2008 in the academic journal *Computers & Education* looked at how these laptops have affected classroom behaviour. "Results showed that students who used laptops in class spent considerable time multitasking and that laptop use posed a significant distraction to both users and fellow students," the research observes. "Most importantly, the level of laptop use was negatively related to several measures of student learning." Students with laptops had lower test results than those without. The reason? They were often not paying attention to their teacher. We should expect the same thing from cellphones.

Similarly, a 2009 study looked at students who sent instant messages during class. Texting students took longer to perform simple tasks such as reading a written passage than those who did not. Consider it another blow to the alleged benefits of multitasking. An investigation into PowerPoint lectures found students enjoyed them more than traditional presentations, although this did nothing to raise test scores. Clickers, small hand-held wireless devices used for in-class quizzes that are popular with students and teachers, similarly have no discernable impact on marks.

Technology Will Never Replace Skilled Teachers

Technology may lower school costs, make marking more efficient and even raise student satisfaction. But it can't produce students with better grades. And this means technology will never replace the timeless need for skilled teachers capable of catching the attention of easily distracted students and engaging their minds. The smartest phones may be the ones we keep outside the classroom.

8

Teaching Students Cell Phone Responsibility Can Begin Early

Liz Kolb

Specializing in education technologies, Liz Kolb is a clinical assistant professor at the University of Michigan School of Education. Kolb is the author of Toys to Tools: Connecting Student Cell Phones to Education.

Cell phones should be introduced in education to promote digital etiquette and responsibility. Educators are in a position to help students—unfamiliar with the consequences of using or misusing technology—navigate through today's media environment. Secondary students are the focus of cell phones and learning, but younger students can also benefit; the number of elementary-age children with them is rapidly growing. Therefore, teaching digital etiquette and responsibility can start early, before children develop poor habits. Similar to driver's education or early exposure to computers, instructing young students in the appropriate uses of cell phones is beneficial.

[A] reason to consider introducing cell phones in learning is to promote digital etiquette, a concept foreign to most people. According to a recent study by the Pew Internet & American Life Project, "How Americans Use Their Cell Phones":

> More than a quarter of cell phone owners (28%) admit they sometimes do not drive as safely as they should while they use their mobile devices. . . . Furthermore, 82% of all Americans and 86% of cell users report being irritated at least occasionally by loud and annoying cell users who conduct their calls in public places. Indeed, nearly one in ten cell phone owners (8%) admit they themselves have drawn criticism or irritated stares from others when they are using their cell phones in public.

An educator's job is to help students navigate and stay safe in their media world. Students are often unaware of and indifferent to the consequences of their use and misuse of technology. Currently, many students do not worry about protecting their own privacy or the privacy of others when using digital media. For example, 55% of students do not care whether the digital material they use is copyrighted. Additionally, only 25% of students consider online safety and cost a concern when using the Internet. When it comes to etiquette, students ages 10–17 often do not seem to understand appropriate cell phone use. According to the Disney Mobile Survey (2007), while nine out of ten 10- to 17-year-olds believe they are polite on their cell phones, 52% admit to sending text messages at the movie theater, while 28% admit to sending text messages at the dinner table. These statistics demonstrate that teens and tweens are unaware of cell phone etiquette, and educators have an opportunity to teach them appropriate uses of this communication device.

Instead of spending time, energy, and money creating policies to fight cell phone use in schools, we are better served by directing our resources toward finding useful ways to integrate these devices as knowledge construction, data collection, and collaborative communication tools, and toward teaching digital etiquette. Parents may appreciate the help. [Research psychologist Larry] Rosen found that only one-third of parents have seen their children's MySpace page and only 16% of them check it on a regular basis. Although this does not relate directly to cell phones, it demonstrates that parents may need some assistance in monitoring their children and teaching them about digital etiquette. . . .

Early intervention may be the key to help students develop appropriate cell phone etiquette and budget management.

Cell Phones in Preschool and Lower Elementary Learning

Although the focus . . . is on cell phones as learning tools for secondary students, cell phones also have potential as learning tools for preschool and elementary students. Although many argue (and it is a valid argument) that PK–5 students do not have their own cell phones, those statistics are rapidly changing. [Marketing analyst Marina] Amoroso estimates that by 2010, 54% of 8–12 year olds will have their own cell phone. [Writer Adam] Hunter describes parents' reasons for giving younger children cell phones: Safety and communication are significant concerns—parents want to be able to keep track of their children at all times. Parents also think cell phones allow them to have a better connection with their children. Cell phones allow parents to call their children at any time to talk about their day.

Although Hunter also found that some parents oppose giving their younger children cell phones, considering the growing number of elementary-age children with cell phones, I think it is reasonable to consider how cell phones could be learning tools for younger students. In addition, educational organizations are starting to research and develop educational software for cell phones targeted at young children. Basic literacy skills such as reading and arithmetic are the focus of these efforts. One example by PBS Kids is called the "Ready to

Learn Cell Phone Study." The researchers loaded parents' cell phones with software designed to help preschoolers learn their alphabet. Ultimately they found that cell phones were effective tools for delivering the PBS preschool Ready to Learn content to preschoolers. Therefore it is not ridiculous to begin to consider how cell phones could be used as learning tools for younger children.

Etiquette Starts Early

[One] big complaint expressed by adults concerning cell phones and teenagers is that they are using them inappropriately. Teenagers are frequently text messaging or talking while they are driving; they text during movies, speeches, and church services; and they often overspend their minutes. By the time students reach the secondary level, they have already developed many poor cell phone habits. Early intervention may be the key to help students develop appropriate cell phone etiquette and budget management. Using a cell phone could be compared to driving a car. While the age to obtain a license in most states is 16, students with parent supervision and certified driving instructors can start learning to drive earlier (usually 15).

Instead of just giving teenagers cell phones for the first time and having them incur overcharges for too much text messaging because they don't understand their phone plans, or getting in trouble at school for taking inappropriate pictures because they were never taught cell phone etiquette, children could be exposed to appropriate uses long before they have their own phone. This could happen under the supervision of teachers and parents. In addition, the cell phone can first be introduced to younger students as a learning tool rather than a social toy.

Additionally, teachers could send home guidelines for parents to help them talk with their children about cell phone etiquette. . . .

Student Ownership

One important aspect to consider is that students themselves do not need to have their own cell phones in order to take advantage of them as learning tools. Keep in mind that most elementary-age children do not own their own computers, yet we do not ignore the fact that the computer can be a useful learning tool for younger students. There are many one-computer classrooms where innovative teachers employ one computer for 30 students; the same can be done for cell phones. If the classroom teacher has a cell phone, that would be enough. Many activities can be done with just one cell phone. It is also unnecessary for students to use cell phones inside the classroom.

9

Children in Elementary School Are Too Young for Cell Phones

Marguerite Reardon

Marguerite Reardon is a senior writer at CNET, where she writes an advice column on technology, "Ask Maggie."

Parents may want to give their elementary or middle school-aged child a cell phone for convenience. But it can become a big distraction by connecting him or her to their friends at all times, so parents may want to hold off until the child is in high school. Experts agree, pointing out that cell phones give kids the opportunity to socialize without supervision. Instead, parents should use an old or simple phone as a "family" phone to be loaned out as needed. As for giving a child a smartphone, the appropriate age is when he or she is already in high school, when parents are comfortable with their child using social networks and having mobile Internet access.

More than 90 percent of Americans own a cellphone today, and a growing number of those cellphone users are children. But how young is too young for a cellphone?

Cellphone or Smartphone for Kids?

Dear Maggie,

This is a two-part question. I'm considering getting a cell-phone for my 11-year old daughter for Christmas. A lot of girls in her class already have phones. She's been begging me for one. But I'm not sure if this is too young. What do you think?

Also, at what age do you think it's appropriate for a child to switch from a regular feature phone to a smartphone? Are there any phones or services you can recommend? And can you offer any advice for preventing overages?

Thanks, Annemarie

Dear Annemarie,

I'm probably a bit more conservative than most people on this subject, but I think it's better to wait as long as possible before giving your child a cellphone.

While I recognize that it can be a nice convenience for busy parents and families with hectic schedules, I think it also can turn into a huge distraction for kids and it opens a whole can of worms in terms of social interaction for children at a time when they may not need to be connected every moment to their peers. And if the only reason you are getting the phone is because her friends have them and she wants to socialize, then I think it's wise to wait.

In particular, I am not a fan of elementary or middle school age children having their own cellphones. And neither are some parenting experts.

"When you give your child a cellphone you are giving him or her a lot more freedom and access to a social life that can't be supervised," said Marybeth Hicks, editor of Family Events, a newsletter for families and moms, and author of two books on parenting. "A lot of parents are blindsided by some things that come up as a result of kids using cellphones, and the truth is they are the ones providing that access."

Hicks, who has four children, said she recommends that kids get their first cellphone in high school.

"Getting a cellphone is a rite of passage in our house," she said. "It's something my kids get in the summer between eighth grade and their freshman year of high school."

Hicks said that giving her children their first cellphone is a sign of their growing independence and maturity that comes along with entering a new chapter of adolescence. It also provides that "electronic" tether to home. Her children know that once they have that cellphone they are expected to call her if they find themselves in a situation in which they aren't comfortable with what's going on around them. With a phone in hand, there's no excuse for not calling mom when they're at a party without any parental supervision or where other kids might be drinking alcohol or doing drugs.

While I don't think that all text messaging between tweens is bad, it's an interaction that you as a parent are not able to monitor in real time.

I mostly agree with Hicks' philosophy, and so I think that 11-years-old is a bit young to give a child a cellphone of her own. Again, I know lots of people do it, and I am not passing judgement. I just think that kids today will have a lifetime of gadgets and cellphones. It won't hurt them to wait another few years before getting one of their own.

Instead, I'd recommend using an old phone or a cheap feature phone as a "family" phone that can be kept on the family cell phone plan for $10 a month and loaned out to any child in the family on an as needed basis.

For example, you might want to give your 11-year old daughter the "family" phone if she is going to the movies or a middle school dance, so she can call you when she needs a ride home. But I think it's probably unnecessary for her to have her own phone to text message her friends. While I don't think that all text messaging between tweens is bad, it's an interaction that you as a parent are not able to monitor in real time.

When Is the Right Age for a Smartphone?

So that's my recommendation for an 11-year-old. But what about older kids? When is it appropriate to get your kid a phone, and when should you consider getting your child a smartphone?

Life was much easier for parents a few years ago when cellphones did one thing, made phone calls. But now with smartphones, kids can get full access to the Internet on their phones. While this can be a great thing, especially for adults, when you're searching for a nearby restaurant or need directions to your doctor's office, as a parent, it adds another element of risk for your children who now have access to all kinds of inappropriate content in their pockets.

If you feel comfortable allowing your child to have open access to the Internet and to social networking sites, such as Facebook and Twitter, on your home computer, then you can consider allowing a smartphone. Again, I would suggest that this kind of access is not appropriate for elementary or middle school children, but more for an older teenager, who is more mature.

It's hard to put an exact age on this, but I'd say that if you follow my philosophy a feature phone would be appropriate as a first cellphone for when a child first enters high school. And a smartphone might be more appropriate for a junior or senior in high school. Again, I think you need to consider the maturity of your child when deciding at what age to allow a smartphone.

With parental controls, you can limit access to services like data, as well as limit when they can access the phone and which numbers they can call.

If you take my advice, be careful when you're shopping for a phone for your child. To complicate matters further, the distinction between regular feature phones and smartphones is quickly fading. And wireless operators are making it more difficult to find bare-bones phones for wireless subscribers. Instead, they are trying to steer customers, whether they are adults or children, into devices that use more data services, which means more access to the Internet and social networking services like Facebook and Twitter.

Not only does it provide access to services and content you may not want your kids accessing, it also costs more money. So beware.

If you can't find the most basic, no-frills cellphone that doesn't offer any access to the Internet while you're shopping for a phone, you can still consider a more souped-up feature phone, or "quick messaging" device. But if you don't want to enable access to the Internet, make sure you check out the parental control options through the carrier you are using to shut off access to the Internet. The bigger nationwide carriers all offer some parental controls, but check out their websites for specifics or ask the salesperson for more information.

With prepaid services, you won't have to worry about your teenager exceeding the talk, texting or data usage limits, since they can't exceed their monthly limit.

These "quick messaging" devices featured on many carrier Websites can be a good choice if you're willing to use the parental controls for several reasons. First, they serve as a perfect gateway between a regular feature phone and a smartphone. With parental controls, you can limit access to services like data, as well as limit when they can access the phone and which numbers they can call.

But as your child matures, you can allow more access through the control Website. So your son or daughter can get more functionality as he or she matures.

The second reason these phones are great is that they are inexpensive to buy and own. Often you can get one for free or for less than $50 with a two-year contract. And if you restrict the data service, you don't need to subscribe to an additional data plan.

These devices also appeal to kids because they come in cool colors, and most of them have full QWERTY keypads or touch screens, which are great for text messaging and accessing social networking sites. . . .

Parental Controls Are Important

Controlling what your child can and cannot access on a smartphone gets a little trickier. Apple has a pretty good set of parental controls for iOS devices, which includes the iPhone. So you could restrict the downloading of certain apps or you could turn off the Safari Internet browser altogether. But you'll still be paying for the data plan. And while voice minutes can be shared in a family plan, data usage cannot. So when you add smartphones to a family plan or you add data to a "quick messaging" feature phone, every line requires its own data plan. And these charges can really add up.

What's more, new smartphone subscribers on AT&T and Verizon Wireless, the two largest wireless providers, cannot get unlimited data service. So there is a risk that your child could run over the usage cap, especially if you're an AT&T subscriber and plan on getting the 200MB plan for $15 a month. (Most users, even kids, should be find with the AT&T 2G service for $25 a month or Verizon's 2GB plan which costs $30 a month.)

If cost is your primary concern, then prepaid services might be a better option for some families. You can get basic feature phones for calling and texting, as well as inexpensive smartphone plans. Services, such as Virgin Mobile and MetroPCS offer full fledged Google Android smartphones for $100 or less. And you can get a plan for as little as $35 a month from Virgin Mobile. The service includes unlimited texting and data with 300 minutes of talk time. MetroPCS offers unlimited voice, texting and data for $40 a month.

With prepaid services, you won't have to worry about your teenager exceeding the talk, texting or data usage limits, since they can't exceed their monthly limit. But the downside is that you won't have the ability to control the service and usage as much through parental control settings as you would through a bigger carrier.

I hope this was helpful. And good luck!

10

Smartphones: Teaching Tool or Brain Candy?

Mark Frydenberg, Wendy Ceccucci, and Patricia Sendall

Mark Frydenberg is a senior lecturer of computer information systems at Bentley University. Wendy Ceccucci is a professor of information systems management at Quinnipiac University. Patricia Sendall is vice provost and professor of management information systems at Merrimack College.

Smartphones are undeniably a permanent feature of college classrooms today. Packed with apps, games, social networking, and media, the devices are the ultimate obsession of college students and can divert their attention from work in the classroom. However, with their impressive computing power and portability, smartphones are a powerful learning tool with many possibilities. Students can use apps in the field to collect and share information. Confined to the classroom, students can use their devices to quickly find information for class discussions, take notes, and participate anonymously. Smartphones, though, do have limitations. For more substantial activities, such as analyzing data or using multimedia editing tools, students must use desktop computers.

Let's get one thing straight. Smartphones are a permanent feature of college classrooms, whether you like it or not. Most students already have them, and it's just a matter of time before the rest follow suit. From ordering a late-night pizza to posting pictures on Facebook of their roommates eating it, students rely on their phones for *everything*.

Yet students' attachment to these devices is not necessarily a bad thing. Like any internet-connected computer, smartphones can play a valuable—even exciting—role in teaching and learning. What better way to reach students than via a device they treat like their significant other? At the same time, smartphones do have a dark side. They are the ultimate obsession of today's students—a wonderland of games, friends, apps, and YouTube videos. Does the bored kid in the back row really need such easy diversions? As educators work to come to terms with these devices, the challenge will be to find ways to accentuate the positives while minimizing the distractions.

Smartphone as Learning Tool

Today's smartphones have the computing power of a mid-1990s personal computer. They *are* computers, and it's time we started thinking of them as such. What's more, they come with the added benefit of being constantly connected to the internet.

What makes them different, obviously, are their tiny size and weight. Today, an iPhone weighs less than 5 ounces and fits in your pocket. Unlike a laptop, it's truly portable. If you don't buy into that, try sprinting to class with a 7-pound laptop smacking you in the kidneys.

Portability is what makes the smartphone such a powerful learning tool. As the concept of the walled classroom breaks down, the smartphone is perfectly suited to support the untethered world of teaching and learning. Students in the field can use the camera to take pictures or videos, the built-in microphone to record interviews, the Oik app to broadcast live video, the browser to perform research, and the keyboard to jot down their notes—anytime, anywhere.

The smartphone's potential as a learning tool is rapidly being discovered by faculty. Paul Wallace, assistant professor of instructional technology at Appalachian State University (NC), taught his students to use the Scvngr application as a way to apply their classroom knowledge to benefit the local community. Students partnered with Watauga River Conservation Partners, a local community organization, to create mobile scavenger hunts to help the community learn about wetlands and conservation. Not only did students learn to use mobile technology, they were also able apply their classroom knowledge in the field.

In many ways, the smartphone is the fast-food restaurant of technology. It's where you go for simple, quick information when you're on the road.

Another demonstration of smartphone-enabled learning is Project Noah, which is based on the premise that students can create and share knowledge using their mobile devices. Students use the app (iPhone or Android) to document and take photos of sighted insects, birds, and bushes, and then share their findings with an online community.

Not a Panacea

Within the confines of a classroom, the smartphone's advantages are obviously more limited. Some instructors are using polling applications such as Poll Everywhere to ask students if they read a particular chapter, or what they found most compelling about it. Instead of raising their hands, students respond by anonymous text message, with their answers appearing on a screen for all to see.

Smartphones also allow students to Google information that can add to class discussions. Gone are the days of frantically flipping through a textbook to find the answers. In addition, in lieu of old-fashioned study guides, students can make their own electronic flash cards using applications such as FlashCards++, Quizlet, or CoboCards.

Instructors have to understand the technology's limitations, however. In many ways, the smartphone is the fast-food restaurant of technology. It's where you go for simple, quick information when you're on the road. When you need something more substantial—data analysis, multimedia editing tools, or software development, for example—it helps to have a more powerful computer, with a full keyboard and large screen. Try taking detailed notes using your thumbs, for example, or using classroom-specific applications such as Quick-Books for accounting or SPSS for statistics. Even if there were apps for that, it would be like looking at the Grand Canyon through a keyhole. You just can't do it.

Minimizing the Distractions

And what of the frivolous flip side of smartphone use? For generations, disengaged students have amused themselves in class with everything from magazines to doodling to full-blown siestas. Compared with the capabilities of the smartphone, though, these are all small ball. The smartphone is the *world* at their fingertips. As exciting and useful as this may be for a motivated student, the smartphone is also the ultimate digital diversion for the disengaged. Among this group, Economics 101 is always going to lose to Angry Birds.

Is there anything lecturers can do to counter the tendency among certain students to zone out with their smartphones? Or is it even the lecturer's responsibility? These are, after all, voting-age adults. They either do the work and succeed, or they goof off and fail.

Even if you take this Darwinian approach, no teacher likes to be ignored, and faculty on campuses nationwide have tried a variety of tactics to control smartphone use in class. One of the most successful is *not* to ask students to put their phones away, but simply to leave them visible on their desks. This discourages students from holding the devices on their laps while they text and tweet away. Indeed, classroom instructors might want to take a page from the airlines, asking students to power off their electronic devices for the duration of the flight.

It would be a mistake, though, to try to close smartphones down altogether. Their educational possibilities are just being unearthed. An increasing number of apps—available free or for a nominal price—are being written for educational purposes. Students can learn everything from mathematics to science, history, and geography. Teaching statistics? There's an app for that.

Nevertheless, instructors should probably avoid using smartphones in each and every class session. The novelty will wear off with overuse, especially if the use is not intuitive. Think about how you already use your smartphone and how those tasks might translate to a classroom setting. If you're comfortable with the technology, the applications will follow.

Organizations to Contact

The editors have compiled the following list of organizations concerned with the issues debated in this book. The descriptions are derived from materials provided by the organizations. All have publications or information available for interested readers. The list was compiled on the date of publication of the present volume; the information provided may change. Be aware that many organizations take several weeks or longer to respond to inquiries, so allow as much time as possible.

American Civil Liberties Union (ACLU)
125 Broad St., 18th Floor, New York, NY   10004
(212) 549-2500
e-mail: aclu@aclu.org
website: www.aclu.org

The American Civil Liberties Union (ACLU) is a national organization that works to defend the civil rights of Americans as guaranteed in the Constitution. It publishes various materials, papers, and blogs on civil liberties, including the national newsletter *Civil Liberties* and a set of handbooks on individual rights. The ACLU defends students' right to privacy on their cell phones, and the organization's website includes a number of pages and legal updates dealing with issues of student privacy in general.

American Federation of Teachers (AFT)
555 New Jersey Ave. NW, Washington, DC   20001
(202) 879-4400
website: www.aft.org

The American Federation of Teachers (AFT) was founded in 1916 to represent the economic, social, and professional interests of classroom teachers. It has more than three thousand local affiliates nationwide, forty-three state affiliates, and more than 1.3 million members. AFT publishes the *PSRP Reporter*, a quarterly newsletter, and provides resources on cell phones for educators, such as *Classroom Tips: Appropriate Uses of Modern Technology*.

CTIA—The Wireless Association

1400 16th St. NW, Suite 600, Washington, DC   20036

(202) 736-3200 • fax: (202) 785-0721

website: www.ctia.org

CTIA is an international nonprofit membership organization that has represented the wireless communications industry since 1984. The association advocates on behalf of its members at all levels of government. CTIA also coordinates the industry's voluntary efforts to provide consumers with a variety of choices and information regarding their wireless products and services. Its "Get Wise About Wireless" program aims to educate middle school students about cell phone use and responsibility, offering a pamphlet for families and a mini-magazine for students.

Electronic Frontier Foundation (EFF)

815 Eddy St., San Francisco, CA   94109

(415) 436-9333 • fax: (415) 436-9993

e-mail: info@eff.org

website: www.eff.org

The Electronic Frontier Foundation (EFF) is an organization of lawyers, policy analysts, activists, technologists, and others that aims to promote a better understanding of telecommunications issues. It fosters awareness of civil liberties issues arising from advancements in computer-based communications media and supports litigation to preserve, protect, and extend First Amendment rights in computing and telecommunications technologies. EFF's publications include the electronic newsletter *EFFector Online*, online bulletins, and articles, including "EFF to Texas High Court: A Cell Phone Isn't a Pair of Pants."

Embrace Civility in the Digital Age

474 W. 29th Ave., Eugene, OR   97405
(541) 556-1145
e-mail: info@embracecivility.org
website: www.embracecivility.org

Formerly the Center for Safe and Responsible Internet Use, Embrace Civility in the Digital Age promotes approaches that address youth well-being and risk in the digital age in a manner that promotes positive norms, increases effective skills and resiliency, and encourages young people to be helpful allies who positively intervene when they witness peers being hurt or at risk. The organization offers reports, issue briefs, and articles online.

National Crime Prevention Council (NCPC)

2001 Jefferson Davis Hwy., Suite 901, Arlington, VA   22202
(202) 466-6272
website: www.ncpc.org

The mission of the National Crime Prevention Council (NCPC) is to be the nation's leader in helping people keep themselves, their families, and their communities safe from crime. To achieve this, NCPC produces tools that communities can use to learn crime prevention strategies, engage community members, and coordinate with local agencies. Its website includes information on cyberbullying and cell phone safety.

National Education Association (NEA)

1201 16th St. NW, Washington, DC   20036-3290
(202) 833-4000 • fax: (202) 822-7974
website: www.nea.org

The National Education Association (NEA), the nation's largest professional employee organization, is committed to advancing the cause of public education. Its three million members work at every level of education—from pre-school to university graduate programs. NEA has affiliate organizations in every state and in more than fourteen thousand communities across the United States. On its website, the association covers the various issues that accompany the use of cell phones in education and by students.

US Department of Education (ED)

400 Maryland Ave. SW, Washington, DC   20202
(800) USA-LEARN (872-5327)
website: www.ed.gov

Established in 1980, the US Department of Education (ED) aims to promote student achievement, establish policies on federal financial aid for education, focus national attention on key educational issues, and prohibit discrimination and ensure equal access to education. The department publishes several newsletters and publications, with numerous articles regarding mobile technology in schools and in education.

Bibliography

Books

Mark Bauerlein   *The Dumbest Generation: How the
Digital Age Stupefies Young Americans
and Jeopardizes Our Future (Or, Don't
Trust Anyone Under 30).* New York:
Jeremy P. Tarcher/Penguin, 2008.

Susan
Brooks-Young, ed.   *Teaching with the Tools Kids Really
Use: Learning with Web and Mobile
Technologies.* Thousand Oaks, CA:
Corwin, 2010.

Gerard Goggin   *Cell Phone Culture: Mobile Technology
in Everyday Life.* New York:
Routledge, 2006.

Andrew Keen   *Digital Vertigo: How Today's Online
Social Revolution Is Dividing,
Diminishing, and Disorienting Us.*
New York: St. Martin's Press, 2012.

Rich Ling and
Scott W. Campell   *Mobile Communication: Bringing Us
Together and Tearing Us Apart.* New
Brunswick, NJ: Transaction
Publishers, 2011.

Susan Maushart   *The Winter of Our Disconnect: How
Three Totally Wired Teenagers (and a
Mother Who Slept with Her iPhone)
Pulled the Plug on Their Technology
and Lived to Tell the Tale.* New York:
Jeremy P. Tarcher/Penguin, 2011.

Charles Miller and Aaron Doering	*The New Landscape of Mobile Learning: Redesigning Education in an App-Based World.* New York: Routledge, 2014.
John Palfry and Urs Gasser	*Born Digital: Understanding the First Generation of Digital Natives.* New York: Basic Books, 2008.
Clark N. Quinn	*The Mobile Academy: mLearning for Higher Education.* San Francisco: Jossey-Bass, 2012.
Larry D. Rosen	*iDisorder: Understanding Our Obsession with Technology and Overcoming Its Hold on Us.* New York: Palgrave Macmillan, 2012.

Periodicals and Internet Sources

Patrick Barkman and Stephen Moss	"Should Mobile Phones Be Banned in Schools?" *Guardian*, November 27, 2012.
John-Paul Dickie	"Why Teenagers and Children Should Be Banned from Using Smartphones Like the BlackBerry or iPhone," PostDesk, December 29, 2011. www.postdesk.com.
Robert Earl	"Do Cell Phones Belong in the Classroom?" *Atlantic*, May 18, 2012.
Berlin Fang	"From Distraction to Engagement: Wireless Devices in the Classroom," *EDUCAUSE Review Online*, December 22, 2009. www.educause.edu.

Sarah Gonzalez   "How Schools Are Coping with a Communications Obsession," StateImpact, August 2, 2012. http://stateimpact.npr.org.

Randi Kaye   "How a Cell Phone Picture Led to Girl's Suicide," CNN, October 7, 2010. www.cnn.com.

Ryan Lytle   "Smartphone Use Among College Students Concerns Some Professors," *US News & World Report*, March 21, 2012.

Anne Michaud   "Instead of Banning Cell Phones, Schools Should Teach Responsible Use," *Newsday*, February 20, 2013.

Brad Moon   "Cellphones in the Classroom: Bad Idea, Inevitable, or Both?" *Wired*, September 20, 2010.

Sarah Pottharst   "Cell Phones: A Classroom Distraction," *Daily Campus*, January 21, 2010.

Kelly Puente   "Mobile Devices Drive Creative Instruction," *District Administration*, February 2012.

Matt Ritchel and Brad Stone   "Industry Makes Pitch That Smartphones Belong in Classroom," *New York Times*, February 15, 2009.

Brian Shane   "Schools Use Smart Devices to Help Make Kids Smarter," *USA Today*, December 28, 2012.

Gerry Smith   "Smartphones Bring Hope, Frustration as Substitute for Computers," *Huffington Post*, June 6, 2012. www.huffingtonpost.com.

Index